DOGS in DISGUISE

Catherine Veitch

QEB

Quarto is the authority on a wide range of topics.

Quarto educates, entertains and enriches the lives of our readers—enthusiasts and lovers of hands-on living.

www.quartoknows.com

Author: Catherine Veitch
Editor: Ellie Brough
Designers: David Ball, Mike Henson
Picture Researcher: Sarah Bell

© 2019 Quarto Publishing plc

First Published in 2019 by QEB Publishing,
an imprint of The Quarto Group.
6 Orchard Road
Suite 100
Lake Forest, CA 92630
T: +1 949 380 7510
F: +1 949 380 7575
www.QuartoKnows.com

A CIP record for this book is available from the
Library of Congress.

ISBN 978-0-7112-4559-4

Manufactured in GuangDong, China TT0619

9 8 7 6 5 4 3 2 1

MIX
Paper from
responsible sources
FSC® C016973

Contents

Introduction

See which lovable breeds of dog you can spot in these doggy disguises. And discover some fun facts along the way.

Dogs come in all shapes and sizes—from tiny fluffballs to magnificent mutts, and from speeding hounds to slouching pooches. Some are slobbering softies, while others are yapping waggy-tails.

These are professional dogs in disguise. Remember: not all dogs like to dress up!

All dogs have their own personalities and no two dogs are the same, even in the same breed. But one thing all dogs have in common is the love a well-cared dog feels toward its owner.

This score is for how good the disguise is.

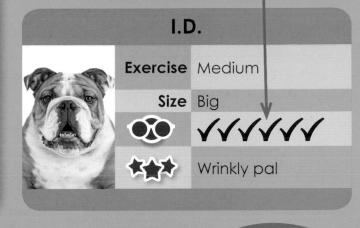

I.D.

Exercise	Medium
Size	Big
👓	✓✓✓✓✓✓
★★★	Wrinkly pal

Check out each dog's I.D.

Airedale Terrier

Your won't have a home covered in fur with an Airedale Terrier as they don't shed much.

I.D.

Exercise	Medium
Size	Big
👓	✓✓
⭐⭐	A good sport

Can you still see me in this disguise?

Well-trained Airedale Terriers are good at many things. They are brave, intelligent, gentle, and eager to please. But watch out when you're out and about with them, as they may zoom off to chase small animals.

Basset Hound

Don't leave smelly socks lying around this pooch. The Basset Hound is a champion sniffer dog!

I.D.

Exercise Medium

Size Small, but chunky

✓✓

Can sniff out anything

Is it dinner time yet?

Basset Hounds' short legs may help them get their noses close to the ground when they're on a scent trail. But being a shortie means they pick up lots of dirt from the ground, so they need many baths!

Beagle

You'll know when a Beagle's nearby—you'll hear its loud barks, yaps, and howls!

Did you call for Wonder-Dog?

I.D.

Exercise	High
Size	Small and squat
⚫⚫	✓✓✓✓✓✓
★★★	Likes you to be around

Beagles are super smellers
and were used for hunting in
packs with other dogs. This
happy-go-lucky breed likes
to have company and can
get down in the dumps if left
on their own for too long.

Bernese Mountain Dog

The beefy Bernese Mountain Dog loves to play and is really a big softie.

I.D.	
Exercise	Medium
Size	Huge
⬤⬤	✓✓✓✓
★★★	A good guard dog

Can I have a cuddle?

Bernese Mountain Dogs need lots of exercise and love being outside. They make great walking buddies. Around the home, when they're not being silly, they are eager to please and will love It If you give them a job to do.

Border Collie

Border Collies are super-smart dogs and the brightest of all breeds.

I.D.

Exercise	High
Size	Medium
👓👓	✓✓
⭐⭐	Brains and beauty

I'm top of the class!

Border Collies need lots of activities to keep their brains and bodies busy. They especially love learning new tricks, and going to dog training and agility classes.

Boxer

Brainy Boxers may invent their own games if they get bored with training.

This is easy-peasy! Woof!

I.D.

Exercise High

Size Big

 ✔✔

 A big dog with a big heart

Boxers have a silly side, too, and don't grow up until they're three years old—that's 21 in human years! When excited, they may stand on their back legs and kick out their front paws, like a human boxer. So it's a good idea to teach them the word "down"!

Cavalier King Charles Spaniel

Sappy Cavalier King Charles Spaniels love nothing better than snuggling on laps.

I.D.	
Exercise	Medium
Size	Small
👓	✓✓✓
★★★	Sweet and loving

This floor isn't as comfy as a lap!

I'm king for the day!

This breed is named after a King Charles who kept them as pets hundreds of years ago. He loved them so much he didn't go anywhere without them. Because they are so friendly, they are not so good at being guard dogs!

Chihuahua

Chihuahuas may be the smallest breed of dog but they make a big impression!

I.D.	
Exercise	Low
Size	Tiny
👀	✓✓
★★★	A good guard dog

Goggles— the best disguise!

Chihuahuas have big personalities. They love being around people and will follow their owners everywhere. They are fun-loving and affectionate, but can be very demanding if they're spoiled!

Chow Chow

Fluffy Chow Chows are not good swimmers. All that fur gets very heavy when it's wet.

I.D.	
Exercise	Medium
Size	Big
👓	✔✔
⭐⭐⭐	Bundle of fluff

How does my hat look?

The blue-tongued Chow Chow (yes, it has a blue tongue!) knows what it wants and can be stubborn. The Chow Chow just needs a firm owner to train it, then it will grow up to be a lovable furry friend.

Cocker Spaniel

Cocker Spaniels' long, floppy ears can pick up bugs and need checking often.

I.D.

Exercise	High
Size	Small
✓✓✓✓
Gentle friend

Time for an ear check!

Cocker Spaniels are full of energy and need lots of exercise. They especially love fetching things so games with a ball are a big hit. Watch out when you're out, as they'll dash off after things!

Corgi

Corgis are a favorite with royalty. The Queen of England has owned over 30 of them!

Do I look cool in these?

I.D.	
Exercise	Medium
Size	Medium
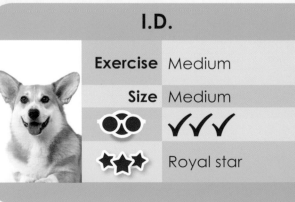	✓✓✓
★★★	Royal star

Don't be fooled by the Corgi's chunky build— these dogs can run very fast when they want to. Corgis were used to herd cattle and would nip at a stray cow's heels to push it back into the group. They are smart, too, and easily learn commands.

Dachshund

Dachshunds are agile little dogs that are good at getting in and out of tight spots.

I.D.	
Exercise	Medium
Size	Tiny
👓	✓✓✓✓✓
★★★	Agile mover

Are you ready to play?

Dachshunds, or Doxies as their friends call them, are famous for their funny shape. But their short legs and long bodies make them easy to love. They live longer than other breeds. The oldest Doxie lived to 21—that's 147 in human years!

Dalmatian

Time to play connect the dots! Dalmatians have spots all over, even inside their mouths!

I.D.

Exercise	High
Size	Big
👓👓	✓✓✓
⭐⭐⭐	Horsey hound

Can you spot me in my disguise?

Dogs may be man's best friend, but Dalmatians are a horse's best friend! They used to run alongside horse-pulled carriages to scare away stray dogs and keep the horses calm. Dalmatians often curl their lips so it looks like they're smiling!

English Bulldog

Hold your nose—it's the windy English Bulldog!

I.D.

Exercise	Medium
Size	Big
⬤⬤	✓✓✓✓✓✓
★★★	Wrinkly pal

Do I really have to wear this?

English Bulldogs fart, snort, and slobber because their short snouts make them gassy. But they don't need much exercise—a run around the garden in the cool part of day will be fine.

French Bulldog

French Bulldogs make charming companions who enjoy cuddling and like to keep cool.

My hat is so in style!

I.D.

Exercise	Low
Size	Small
⊙⊙	✓✓✓✓✓
★★★	Chatty chap

French Bulldogs don't bark as much as other breeds so they won't upset the neighbors. But they do like to talk in their own way, as they yawn, yip, and gargle. They may even sing along with you!

German Shepherd

German Shepherds are busy dogs who like to be given jobs.

I.D.

Exercise	High
Size	Huge
👀	✓✓✓✓
★★★	A good guard dog

Now for my next patient...

German Shepherds are good at obeying commands. Many of these dogs work with the police. They make great guard dogs in the home, too! With proper training there's not much a German Shepherd can't do!

Golden Retriever

Golden Retrievers are fantastic at fetching and love carrying things in their mouths.

I.D.

Exercise	High
Size	Big
👓	✓✓✓
★★	Furry friend

I'm dreaming about playing ball!

Golden Retrievers have a special double coat that keeps them warm in the winter and cool in the summer. Their coat is also waterproof, which is handy as they like splashing around in the water!

Great Dane

Great Danes are big softies who love chilling out at home.

I.D.

Exercise High

Size Huge

✓✓✓✓

Gentle giant

Do I smell nice?

Great Danes don't ask for a lot. After a daily walk, they are happy just to flop down and cuddle with you. If you don't want these huge gentle giants climbing onto furniture and your lap, it's best to train them when they are pups.

Greyhound

With their strong back legs and long, lean bodies, Greyhounds are built for speed.

I.D.	
Exercise	Medium
Size	Big
👀	✓✓✓
★★★	Rocket power

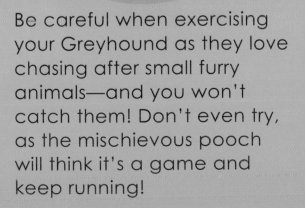

Because I'm worth it!

Be careful when exercising your Greyhound as they love chasing after small furry animals—and you won't catch them! Don't even try, as the mischievous pooch will think it's a game and keep running!

Irish Setter

Irish Setters need brushing often to keep their beautiful coats silky soft.

I.D.	
Exercise	High
Size	Big
👓	✓✓
★★★	Cheeky chap

Can you play with me?

Irish Setters are full of energy and can be a little bit bonkers! So they need lots of exercise and things to do in the home to keep them out of mischief and calm them down. Then they'll be happy, fun-loving doggies.

Irish Wolfhound

Towering Irish Wolfhounds may look scary, but they are too gentle to be guard dogs.

I.D.	
Exercise	High
Size	Huge
👓	✓✓✓✓
⭐⭐⭐	Big and beautiful

Read all about me!

Irish Wolfhounds are big dogs with big dogs' needs. They need to live in homes with lots of space inside and outside, they eat a lot, and it costs a lot to take them to the vet or kennels. When they're sick, they still need cuddles and you need to be strong to pick them up!

Jack Russell Terrier

Lively Jack Russell Terriers like lots of attention and keeping busy all day long!

I.D.

Exercise Medium

Size Tiny

✓✓✓✓✓

Ball of energy

Let's go on an adventure!

Jack Russells love to run around, sniff, and explore outdoors. You'll need a very high fence around your yard as they can jump very high. They are also expert diggers so make sure the fence goes below ground, too!

Labradoodle

Labradoodles are part Labrador and part Poodle. Can you guess which parts?

I.D.

Exercise	High	
Size	Small, medium, big	
👓	✓✓✓	
★★★	A cuddly teddy bear	

I'm ready for a super walk!

Labradoodles are playful and ready for adventure. Their curly coat is the Poodle part. This type of coat doesn't shed much so it's good for people who have allergies to dog hair.

Labrador

Many Labradors are good at keeping their cool, and often have jobs helping people.

I'm Super-Lab, here to help!

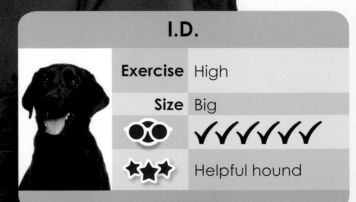

I.D.	
Exercise	High
Size	Big
👀	✓✓✓✓✓
⭐⭐⭐	Helpful hound

When Labradors see water they may dive right in as they love it. Their coat is waterproof, and they are good swimmers as their feet are webbed, like a duck. Just stand back when they come out!

Lhasa Apso

Lhasa Apsos may be tiny, but they make great guard dogs with their loud, sharp barks!

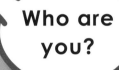

Who are you?

I.D.

Exercise Low

Size Tiny

✓✓✓✓

★★★ A good guard dog

With all that hair it's sometimes difficult to see which is the head end of the Lhasa Apso! Brushing this dog to keep it clean and tangle-free is a big job for owners. These dogs are shy with strangers, so it helps to introduce them to lots of people when they're pups.

Newfoundland

The big, cuddly Newfoundland loves a daily walk and a swim to keep fit.

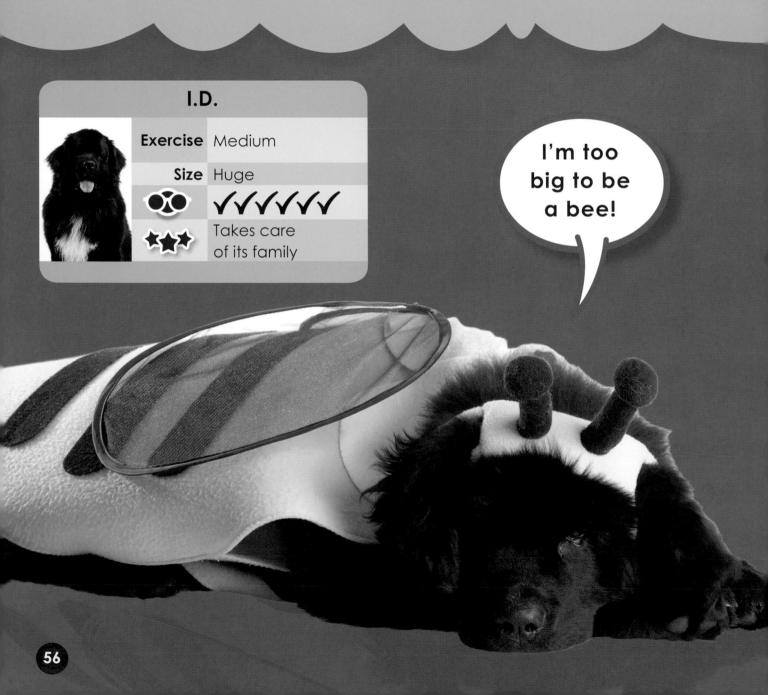

I.D.

Exercise	Medium
Size	Huge
👀	✓✓✓✓✓✓
★★★	Takes care of its family

I'm too big to be a bee!

Newfoundlands are brave dogs and good swimmers. They were bred to rescue people who had fallen into water. They can also sniff out people trapped under snow. Handy to have around!

Old English Sheepdog

Old English Sheepdogs have heavy, woolly coats which need brushing every day.

I.D.	
Exercise	High
Size	Big
👓	✓✓
⭐⭐⭐	Likes to have a laugh

I'm having a bad hair day!

Old English Sheepdogs also need a lot of exercise every day and do best in wide open spaces. But if you make time for your Sheepdog, you will have a funny, happy-go-lucky bundle of joy.

I'm so cool!

Papillon

Papillons may be tiny but they are not shy, and love being around people.

I.D.	
Exercise	Low
Size	Tiny
👓	✓✓✓✓
★★★	Busy doggy

Do I look cute in this disguise?

Papillons are smart and may twist you around their little paws if you're not careful. So it's important to train them and let them meet other dogs and people when they're young. They also have lots of energy and like to keep busy.

Pekingese

Pekingese love city life! They don't need much exercise so they are suited to apartment living.

I'm ready to snuggle on a lap!

I.D.

Exercise	Low
Size	Tiny
◯◯	✓✓
★★★	A good lap dog

A short walk outside in good weather is enough for a Pekingese. They don't like it if it's too hot or too cold. Little Pekingese also have a bark much bigger than their size and make heroic guard dogs!

Pomeranian

These fluffy-faced Pomeranians are often called Poms by their owners.

I.D.

Exercise	Low
Size	Tiny
👀	✓✓✓✓
⭐⭐⭐	Loves attention

This disguise is fishy!

Poms are playful and love being the center of attention. But because Poms are so tiny they don't make great play pals for very young children who might accidentally step on them or play too roughly with them.

Poodle

Poodles' fur never stops growing so they need regular visits to the salon!

I.D.

Exercise	Medium
Size	Tiny, small, medium
👀	✓✓
⭐⭐⭐	Pampered pooch

This outfit is soft like me.

Poodles are super swimmers as they were bred to fetch birds from the water. People used to shave the Poodles' fur in places as too much fur would get very wet and make it hard to swim. Poodles don't have much of a wet-doggie smell!

Pug

Pugs aren't yappy dogs, but make up for it with wheezing, snoring, and snorting!

I.D.	
Exercise	Low
Size	Tiny
👓	✓✓✓✓
⭐⭐	Forever friend

I'm all dressed up to party!

Pugs like short walks but are not very fast and tire easily. So they are perfect companions for city dwellers. Crinkly-faced Pugs are adorable but those wrinkles need daily cleaning!

Rottweiler

The loyal Rottweiler loves to follow you around the home.

I.D.

Exercise High

Size Huge

✓✓✓✓✓✓
Likes it by your side

I only have eyes for you!

Rottweilers are also called Rotties. They are strong dogs. But with the correct training from a young age they will be loving and well-behaved. Taking them to puppy classes is a great way for them to meet other dogs.

Rough Collie

At the end of a day's work or play a Rough Collie will be happy by its owner's side.

I.D.

Exercise	Medium
Size	Big
	✓✓✓✓
★★★	Fluffy furball

Can you guess my disguise? Ho, ho!

Rough collies are smart pups and love learning new tricks. They are gentle dogs and learn best when given treats and cuddles when they're good. They get bored easily, so keep those new tricks coming!

Saint Bernard

Saint Bernards may be gentle giants, but watch out for all that slobber!

I.D.

Exercise	Medium
Size	Massive
	✓✓
	Gentle giants

I'm off to build a snowman!

Saint Bernards come from the snowy Swiss Alps. They're used to the cold— their thick, waterproof coat keeps them warm and dry. They are prone to drool so keep a cloth handy to stay dry during cuddles!

Samoyed

You can't help smiling when you look at a Samoyed as it looks like it's smiling back!

I.D.

Exercise	High
Size	Medium
⊙⊙	✓✓✓
★★★	Smily friend

A smile for the camera!

Samoyeds don't really have a doggy smell, so they don't need baths often. But they do need brushing every day. And once a year they shed their coats. Some owners collect all the shedded soft fur and weave it into clothes!

Schnauzer

Schnauzers are little dogs with big voices and may often bark.

I.D.

Exercise Medium

Size Small

✓✓✓

★★★ Beardy beauty

I'm a unicorn! Woof!

Schnauzers were used to catch rats so keep any small furry pets away from them. The Schnauzer's bushy face protected it from a nasty rat's bite. They also have very good hearing so don't try creeping past them!

Scottish Terrier

Scottish Terriers are tough terriers and have been called a big dog in a little dog's body!

I.D.

Exercise	Medium
Size	Small
	✔✔
	Bold and brave

Ready for action!

Scottish Terriers are also called Scotties. They are loving with their family but can take time to get to know new people. Scotties are good at digging. So be careful as they may dig under a fence or dig up your flowers if they get bored!

Shar Pei

Wrinkly-faced Shar Peis may look adorable but their gentle skin needs special care.

I.D.	
Exercise	Medium
Size	Medium
👓👓	✓✓
⭐⭐⭐	Delicate doggy

Will you look after me?

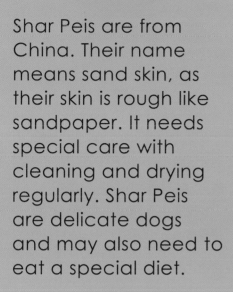

Shar Peis are from China. Their name means sand skin, as their skin is rough like sandpaper. It needs special care with cleaning and drying regularly. Shar Peis are delicate dogs and may also need to eat a special diet.

Shiba Inu

Shiba Inus keep themselves super-clean and even don't like stepping in puddles!

I.D.

Exercise	Medium
Size	Small
	✓✓✓
	Squeaky clean

Chasing birds is more fun!

A Shiba Inu wails like a person when it is upset. Especially when you give them a bath or trim their toenails! Watch that they don't run away outdoors as they like to hunt birds and other creatures.

Siberian Husky

Get ready for Siberian Huskies who have tons of energy and love to run and play!

I.D.

Exercise	High
Size	Medium
✓✓✓✓	
★★★	Top runner

Huskies love being around other dogs and a woofy brother or sister will make them happy. They are not so fond of cats. Make sure your home is fenced as huskies like to wander off and explore.

Do these glasses make me look cool?

Tibetan Mastiff

Lovable, friendly, and extremely fluffy—Tibetan Mastiffs just want to be your best friend.

I.D.

Exercise	Medium
Size	Massive
👀	✓✓✓✓
⭐⭐⭐	Fluffy friend

I love sofa cuddles.

Tibetan Mastiffs are very loyal and loving to their owners and make brilliant companion dogs. They are patient and understanding, but can also be very stubborn! So make sure your mastiff knows who's boss!

Weimaraner

If you're looking for a dog to share the sofa with, Weimaraners are not for you.

I.D.

Exercise	High
Size	Big
👓	✓✓✓✓✓✓
⭐⭐⭐	Busy bee

I like
to keep
busy.

Weimaraners need lots of exercise and space to run around. They're also smart and like to be kept busy. Otherwise they get bored and could get up to mischief, making a mess, stealing treats, or even escaping!

Whippet

Whippets feel the cold more than other dogs so they need coats when it's chilly outside!

Sail away with me!

I.D.	
Exercise	Medium
Size	Small
👓	✓✓✓✓
⭐⭐	Snuggle buddy

Whippets are super-speedy and love to go out for a fast run a couple of times a day. But once a whippet has had a run, it loves to snuggle up for a snooze somewhere warm like a sofa or a bed. They especially love it if you are there, too!

Yorkshire Terrier

Yorkshire Terriers are little dogs with big personalities!

I.D.

Exercise	Low
Size	Tiny
👓	✓✓✓✓✓
⭐⭐	Hairy hound

Do I look cute in this disguise?

Yorkshire Terriers are also called Yorkies. Yorkies can bark a lot so it's best to train them not to bark when they're pups. Yorkies don't shed their hair, so they need trimming regularly. Otherwise it will keep on growing!

Photo credits

(t=top, b=bottom, l=left, r=right, c=center, fc=front cover, bc=back cover)

Shutterstock

fct chrisbrignell, fcb Georgy DZyura, bc 14r 20r 23 cynoclub, 1 Javier Brosch, 2 6r 33 56b 73 WilleeCole Photography, 4-5 5t 32r Susan Schmitz, 6l Dmitry Kalinovsky, 8l Viorel Sima, 10r Antonov Roman, 12r Tugol, 14l 18t 30l 40r 48l 52r 56t 58l 68r 74t 82t 92r 94l Eric Isselee, 16b Gelpi, 19 Kuban_girl, 20t 21 MirasWonderland, 22t 36r 37 46t 54r 62r Jagodka, 22b Nikolai Tsvetkov, 24b Ermolaev Alexander, 24t PardoY, 25 Elayne Massaini, 28r Gorlov Alexander, 64t Justinboat, 31 Sergey Fatin, 34t 88t Svetography, 36l Roger costa morera, 38t Irina oxilixo, 42l fivespots, 18b 44t Dora Zett, 50l Megan Betteridge, 50r Picture-Pet, 54l Annette Shaff, 57 D. Ribeiro, 60t Anna Mandrikyan, 64b Robin Yu, 70l Djomas, 71 Linn Currie, 72r Erik Lam, 76l GPPets, 78l Andreina Nunez, 78r Maximilian100, 80t Kasefoto, 83 Istvan Csak, 84t Seregraff, 85 Lyudvig Aristarhovich, 86l Africa Studio, 86r ANURAK PONGPATIMET, 88r PonomarenkoNataly, 89 dien, 90l Csanad Kiss

Alamy

11 MANDY GODBEHEAR, 13 38b 47 75 90r Juniors Bildarchiv GmbH, 15 Life on white, 34b Gina Kelly, 39 Ken Howard, 61 Iuliia Mashkova, 65 ZUMA Press Inc, 68l imageBROKER, 74, 80b bonzami Emmanuelle, 76r 79 TongRo Images, 77 LightField Studios Inc., 91 Panther Media GmBH, 95 Katrina Brown

Getty

7 Melissa Ross, 9 70r GK Hart, 10l joshblake, 12l GlobalP, 16t jhorrocks, 17 walik, 26l Jne Valokuvaus, 27 46b alkir, 28l Karen Brodie, 29 35 retales botijero, 30r Fuse, 32l Winnie Au, 40 Catherine Ledner, 41 Kathy Rangel / FOAP, 42r DogPhoto. com, 43 Lee Towndrow, 44r LSOphoto, 55 IvonneW, 58r danilobiancalana, 60b EnchantedFairy, 62l Dan Hallman, 63 Alex Sharp, 66r H. Armstrong Roberts, 69 Monica Click, 72l delectus, 81 Mehmen Zelkovic, 82r anniepaddington, 84l BLOOMimage, 87 Sergeeva, 92l 93 Rainer Elstermann, 94r ViewStock